HOW TO KILL A BAD MAN

Copyright © 2018 by Josh Hyde

Without limiting the rights under copyright, no part of this publication may be reproduced, stored in or introduced into a retrieval system, or transmitted, in any form or by any means (electronic, mechanical, photocopying, recording, or otherwise), without the prior written permission of both the copyright owner and the publisher of this book.

ISBN: 978-1-936955-24-4

Layout by Nathaniel Kennon Perkins
Cover photo by Sarah Hyde
Story editor: Mitch Shenassa

Published by Bäuu Press
Golden, CO
www.bauuinstitute.com

HOW TO KILL A BAD MAN

a screenplay
by Josh Hyde

Bäuu Press
Golden, CO

Introduction

I'm aging. And so are you. But let's imagine.

Imagine, if you can, that you're a 17-year old version of this aging me. You've actually finished high school, taken out a shitload of loans to pay for college in Chicago, and you're full of the naive dreams of a working class kid who thinks he's got the grift figured out. After all, it's graduation night and you and your buddies have an ounce of weed and you're parked at the reservoir, going over all the mad capers you're gonna pull. All the girls you're gonna pull. All the art you're gonna make. All the world you're gonna change or burn down trying to change. Your buddy is going to make films. You're gonna write stories. But first, you gotta go out and live those stories. It's all in front of you. And you've got a whole ounce of sinsamilla to smoke up tonight. And no matter how much you smoke and dream, you couldn't have known.

You couldn't have known this grand heist would find you sprinting for your life through the streets of Guanajuato, Mexico, a bad man behind you who wants it all from you—your wallet, your shoes, your t-shirt, your life. You ran and you made it. You've kept running all this time.

You couldn't have known this grand tour would link you up with the Revolutionary Communist Youth Brigade, South Side Chapter and take you to deliver groceries to the Robert Taylor Homes, that long demolished vertical ghetto of Chicago. You didn't know then that the warnings to leave before the snipers posted up was real talk.

You couldn't have known you'd be documenting Ayahuasca tourism in Peru, following bourgeois spiritual seekers into the mountains with your camera equipment. You didn't know you'd quietly watch as shamans revealed ancient secrets for a fee. You couldn't have guessed it would be to extract your own fee in service to those once smoky dreams, now coming into clearer focus.

You couldn't have known you'd be a part-time smuggler, disguised as a bachelor party, sailing the Ionian Sea between gorgeous Greek Islands. Delivering kilos while having a great time, cash on the barrel head, your risks were ridiculous. You were expecting a child at home. You couldn't have known the lengths you'd go to.

Finally, you couldn't have known that through the smoke of all that weed, a substance that could have cost you the very start in life you were celebrating, you would find yourself in a burgeoning economic marijuana powerhouse in rural Colorado at a time when only dreamers and bad men were taking the gamble.

You couldn't have known that these would be the stories you made and lived when you were looking back, ready to pull that last great heist. But here you are.

At the start of Stanley Elkin's Novel *A Bad Man*, the titular character is bent over his safe with his gorgeous secretary, ready to count his take for the day when into the office walks "a young man in an almost brimless fedora." The young man points a gun and says, "Reach, the jig is up, Feldman." The woman hits the alarm, thinking it's a robbery, but Feldman knows. "What is it?" the woman asks.

"It's the jig," Feldman explained, "It's up."

Friends, I want you to reach. Josh Hyde has burst into the office. He's got the stories. He knows what we've seen. He knows how to kill a bad man. The jig is up. And he wants—no, deserves—everything that's in that safe.

- Ammon Torrence

How to Kill a Bad Man

EXT. MOUNTAIN TOPS - LATE AFTERNOON

Snow covered mountain peaks line the horizon.

A dirt road cuts through the peaks, partially hidden. Still.

A van appears, leaving a trail of dust as the soft sun light calms the day.

EXT. VAN - CONTINUOUS

OSCAR, 25, a nerdy looking hippie, drives the van as SHANA, 23, Latina, thin, sits shotgun. Scrapes and bruises cover her face.

Shana and Oscar are silent. Disheveled. Breathing slowly.

They exchange glances, and Oscar scans the horizon. Searching.

              OSCAR
    I remember a pull-off.

Shana's hands fidget. Nervous.

Oscar notices, and puts a calming hand on her knee.

EXT. DIRT PULL OFF - CONTINUOUS

The van pulls off the main dirt road onto a turnoff.

EXT. MOUNTAIN LOOKOUT WITH TREES - CONTINUOUS

A shovel hits the ground.

A pickaxe hits the ground.

Shana and Oscar dig a hole, seemingly the size of a human body.

Josh Hyde

The mountains surround them. Stillness.

EXT. VAN - CONTINUOUS

Shana and Oscar take full, lumpy black trash bags out of the van.

EXT. MOUNTAIN LOOK OUT WITH TREES - CONTINUOUS

Shana and Oscar toss the trash bags into the hole.

They struggle to carry the last trash bag. It's the size of a human torso.

The hole is full.

Clods of dirt fall, covering the trash bags.

Oscar looks at the freshly dug dirt. Uneasy.

He walks around, searching for something. Shana watches him.

He picks up a rock, looks at it, decides it's too small.

He tosses it aside and continues to look.

He finds another rock, strains to pick it, walks toward Shana.

EXT. MOUNTAIN LOOKOUT WITH TREES - MOMENTS LATER

Stones cover the grave, concealing the fresh dirt.

It's done.

They sit on the pile of stones, staring at the horizon.

The clouds reflect the sun as the sky unfolds.

> OSCAR
> No one is gonna' miss him.

How to Kill a Bad Man

Shana looks at Oscar, finding a sense of peace.

He puts his arm around her, pulling her close.

She feels safe, nestles into him.

> FLASHBACK TO.

EXT. HOUSE - MORNING

A black compact car, missing a hubcap or two, pulls up to a one-story house.

Shana parks and grabs a shoulder bag from the back seat. Her face is spotless, no scratches or bruises.

She tosses a pair of small Japanese bonsai scissors in her bag, before slinging it over her arm and locking the car.

Oscar exits the house, carrying a bag, walking to a white minivan.

He stops, checking the bag for something. He finds a small container with amber-colored balls of hash.

> OSCAR
> I got a surprise for us at the end of the day.

Shana meets Oscar at the van. They get in.

> SHANA
> I hate surprises.

Oscar looks at his phone for directions.

> OSCAR
> Damn, this homie lives deep in the mountains.

> SHANA
> How's the dispensary?

He looks up from his phone, putting the keys in the ignition.

Josh Hyde

                    OSCAR
          The warehouse cut my hours to a
          couple days a week.

Oscar searches through his pockets, taking out his Medical Marijuana Enforcement Division badge.

                    OSCAR (CONT'D)
          You got your badge?

                    SHANA
          Do I need it?

Oscar nods, "Yeah."

                    OSCAR
          Homie wants to see them to make
          sure we're legit.

Shana rolls her eyes and gets out of the van.

She runs to her car, grabbing her badge, along with a big glass pipe from the glove compartment.

She returns, gets back in the van.

                    SHANA
          It's the machines.

Oscar starts the van, flipping through his phone for driving music.

                    SHANA (CONT'D)
          The "triminators"

                    OSCAR
          They're not that bad, I like my
          hands not hurting at the end of a
          shift.

Shana rolls down the window, BLOWING the ashes out of the pipe.

                    SHANA
          Gross, the machines put oil all
          over the buds.

She breaks up a bud in her hand, tosses the stem out of the window.

                    SHANA (CONT'D)
        What's the point of even growing
        it? That oil has to cause cancer.

She loads the pipe with weed.

She takes the Japanese bonsai scissors out of her bag.

                    SHANA (CONT'D)
        Fuck the triminator. All you need
        is these guys right here.

Shana holds them up, cutting through the air.

                    SHANA (CONT'D)
        Easy on the hands and samurai sword
        sharp. I almost cut off the tip of
        my finger.

Shana puts the scissors back in her bag.

Oscar finds the right music, pressing play as a FUNK instrumental emanates from the speakers.

Shana bobs her head.

She takes a hit from the bowl as Oscar pulls out of the driveway.

She turns up the volume as the HORNS brighten the day.

Oscar takes a hit, driving through a family neighborhood.

EXT. NEIGHBORHOOD ROAD - MORNING

The van drives toward the mountains.

                    SHANA
        You wanna' come to Cali with me?

Oscar smiles, nodding, "Yes."

SHANA (CONT'D)
I'm gonna' make 20 grand, get a
house, blow it up, and practice my
hoop all winter.
(looking at Oscar,
smiling)
And then do festivals the rest of
the year.

EXT. MOUNTAIN HIGHWAY - MORNING

The road shifts into a two-lane mountain highway.

SHANA
Is this guy a weirdo?

OSCAR
All these guys are weirdos.
(smiling)
Click and Clack hooked up the work.
He's supposed to be a dick, but he
pays twenty an hour when we're
done.

EXT. SMALL MOUNTAIN ROAD - MORNING

The van turns off the highway to a curvy two lane county road, leading up.

A UFO rises out of trees, flies across the horizon and disappears.

EXT. CURVY MOUNTAIN ROAD - MORNING

The van swerves up the mountain following the road.

FLASHBACK TO.

INT. DISPENSARY TRIM TABLE - DAY

Shana sits at a large conference table with a badge around her neck.

How to Kill a Bad Man

The badge reads, Colorado Medical Marijuana Division of Enforcement. Shana Marie #13645J

Shana watches six trimmers standing around a table, working.

MARTIN, early 60's, a fit, tall Jewish man with a greying beard.

CLICK and CLACK, early 20's, two extremely stoned show kids with flat-brimmed hats.

ANDREW, mid 20's, bearded and weathered from living the musician's lifestyle in Alabama.

LUCY, 30's, an ex-stripper with breast implants, rebuilding her life with a day job.

And Oscar, the newbie, sits at the table, slowly trimming. He watches the other trimmers, learning on the job.

A badge hangs around Oscar's neck. It reads, "Visitor."

Shana eyes Oscar as he massacres the bud in his hand.

She gets up, circles the table, looking through the finished buds in a large aluminum turkey pan. Quality control.

Oscar tosses his bud into the turkey pan.

Shana picks up his bud for inspection. It's barely trimmed, like a 1970's shag carpet.

She looks at Oscar.

     SHANA
 Hey new guy?...
  (looking at the other trimmers)
 Click, what's the new guy's name?

Click looks up from his hands trimming a bud. Eyes red.

     CLICK
 W-h-at?

                        ANDREW
                  (Southern accent)
            Dude, his name can't be "What."

                         LUCY
             There is no way he's Vietnamese.

Lucy and Andrew high five each other, laughing at the joke.

                         CLICK
                I know his name isn't "What."

                         LUCY
                  (whispering to Shana)
             Whatever he is, he's kind of cute.

Shana smiles, agreeing.

                        SHANA
                What's the newbie's name?

Click slowly turns his head to Clack.

                        CLACK
                  What's his badge say?

Click grabs Oscar's badge.

                        CLICK
                Visitor. His name is Visitor.

Oscar tries to speak, but Click puts his finger over Oscar's lips, "Shhhhh."

                        CLACK
                  I think it's European.

Shana laughs to herself, waiting for his name.

                        CLICK
                     The slow guy...

                         LUCY
                 He looks like a Fred.

How to Kill a Bad Man

                ANDREW
Nope. His name begins with a vowel.

Andrew's eyes are squinty and red. Stoned.

            ANDREW (CONT'D)
He's got that look.
  (eyeing Oscar)
AaaaEeeeeeIiiiiiiOoooooooUuuuuuuu.

                CLICK
Shhhhhh. I'm psychic.

Click closes his eyes, focusing.

The table gets quiet, growing into awkward silence.

             CLICK (CONT'D)
  (opening his eyes)
It's Paul. You're a Paul.

              MARTIN
No way dude. He's not a Paul.

               OSCAR
It's Oscar.

                CLICK
Duuuuude, I had three more guesses
left...
  (frowning)
And new European dude...
  (reading the badge again)
Visitor...One of them was Oscar.

Everyone laughs.

                SHANA
Oscar.

Oscar looks at Shana as she holds up his half-trimmed bud.

             SHANA (CONT'D)
Make sure to get all the crows
feet.

Shana turns a bud upside down, finding the largest leaf. It looks like a crow's foot.

Oscar watches her scissors cut off the leaves, "She's cute, naturally beautiful."

> SHANA (CONT'D)
> Then shape it from the bottom.

Shana uses one hand to rotate the bud like a small ball in her hand. As the bud rotates, she trims off the remaining leaves.

Oscar watches the demonstration. Attracted.

> SHANA (CONT'D)
> Got any questions "slow-new guy?"

Oscar smiles at Shana, "No."

Shana smiles back, hiding her attraction.

> FLASHBACK END.

EXT. UNPAVED MOUNTAIN ROAD - DAY

The van drives on a dirt road, nestled between mountain peaks.

> SHANA (O.C.)
> I'm serious about coming to Cali with me.

Oscar is quiet.

> OSCAR (O.C.)
> It sounds fun, but I'm trying to get into law school.

EXT. DIRT ROAD WITH PINES - DAY

The dirt road narrows between rows of pines.

> SHANA
> I can't do school.

The van continues on the road, revealing endless mountain peaks.

How to Kill a Bad Man

>   SHANA (CONT'D)
>   My mom did too much coke when she
>   was pregnant, so my brain doesn't
>   go well with reading.
>   (taking a hit, blowing it
>   out)
>   But I'll need a good lawyer when
>   I'm a baller.

Shana smiles at Oscar.

The dirt road narrows as the van passes a "No Trespassing" sign.

EXT. GEODESIC DOME HOUSE - DAY

Dogs scatter around WAYNE, a wiry, energized, "ping-pong ball" of a red neck, standing in the driveway.

He's worn from years of living hard. He might be 30 going on 50.

He looks around, drinking a beer. He takes out a vial of coke, SNIFFING some straight out of the vial.

He takes a deep breath, inhaling the mountain air.

Wayne lights a cigarette as a white van APPROACHES.

EXT. VAN - DAY

The van slowly pulls up to the geodesic dome house, overlooking a valley. It's perfect.

>   SHANA (O.S.)
>   If I had this spot, I'd never
>   leave.

Oscar and Shana notice Wayne, staring them down.

>   SHANA (CONT'D)
>   What's he on?

>   OSCAR
>   Definitely not sleep.

The van parks.

Wayne waives, "Hello," with his beer. He tosses the cigarette on the ground, putting it out with his foot.

They get out of the van.

>   WAYNE
> Ya'll a little early. I lik' dat'.

>   SHANA
> I'm Shana.

Oscar nods, shaking hands with Wayne.

>   OSCAR
> I'm O.

>   WAYNE
> Is dat' your full name? O? Or is
> dat' lik' a code name?

Wayne eyes Oscar.

>   WAYNE (CONT'D)
> Can I call you Mr. Vowel?

Wayne laughs to himself. Oscar is not amused.

>   WAYNE (CONT'D)
> Y'all 'er a cute couple.
>   (talking to himself)
> Click and Clack did alright.

Wayne waives his hands around.

>   WAYNE (CONT'D)
> This is it. Mountains, house,
> cars, stupid dogs, and the garden.

Wayne points out a garage-shed like building, taking out a cell phone.

>   WAYNE (CONT'D)
> Y'all got your badges?

How to Kill a Bad Man

Shana and Oscar hand their badges to Wayne.

Wayne takes a photo of them with his phone.

     OSCAR
  Why do you need the badges?

     WAYNE
  I like badges. Makes me feel safe.

Wayne hands them back to Shana and Oscar.

     WAYNE (CONT'D)
   (laughing to himself)
  Click and Clack did alright.

The three walk toward the garage-like building, disappearing inside.

         FLASHBACK TO.

EXT. PARKING LOT - AFTERNOON

Oscar walks through a parking lot with the group of trimmers - Shana, Lucy, Martin, Andrew, Click and Clack.

They carry lunches in paper bags and tupperware containers.

     CLICK
  There are cameras around the whole
  building.

Click points out the various cameras to Oscar.

     CLACK
  No bueno.

     CLICK
  We found a secret place to eat
  lunch.

The group walks past the building, disappearing behind a row of bushes.

EXT. RAILROAD TRACKS - AFTERNOON

The group sits on a pile of aging railroad ties.

Click is smoking a bowl, passing it to Clack.

          CLICK
It's got scissor hash on top.

Clack takes a hit as Oscar sits in the middle of the group.

          CLACK
        (blowing hash smoke in
        Oscar's face)
How'd you get hired?

Oscar is quiet, thinking of an answer.

          CLICK
Are you a spy?

          OSCAR
Spy?

          CLACK
I can smell a lie. I'm from Texas.

          CLICK
Are you making the decision to
bring in the machines?

Oscar nods, "No."

          OSCAR
What machines?

          CLACK
Once the machines get here...

          CLICK
It's over.

          OSCAR
Like terminator?

          CLACK
Bro, are you high? Terminator was
a movie.

>   (looking into Oscar's
>   eyes)
>   All of this...Us...You...Me...Over.

Clack slowly opens his arms, motioning to the world around them.

>   CLACK (CONT'D)
>   Once the triminators get here...

>   CLICK
>   It's over.

Click stares down Oscar, "It's over."

>   END FLASHBACK.

INT. GROWING SHACK - DAY

A table, a stereo, and a couch fill a decaying room made of cheap plywood. The windows are warped from years of hot and cold.

The floors are linoleum, worn through to the wood subfloor.

A row of empty hangers lines the wall.

>   WAYNE
>   Y'all're gonna' be trimmin' at the
>   table. I'll bring the plants out.

Wayne stares them down, sizing them up.

>   WAYNE (CONT'D)
>   Y'all don't look too fast.

>   SHANA
>   (brandishing her scissors)
>   I've been trimming in Cali for the
>   last 5 summers. I can do a pound
>   of dry weed in 3 hours, if you grow
>   it right.

Wayne listens, nodding his head. He looks at Oscar.

>   WAYNE
>   What 'bout you Mr. O?

                    OSCAR
          I've been working in the
          dispensaries for the last two
          years.

Wayne looks at Oscar and Shana. Unimpressed.

                    SHANA
          Just tell us what you want and
          we'll get it done.

Shana flexes her trimming arm.

                    SHANA (CONT'D)
          Check these guns out.

Wayne checks out her muscles, eventually settling on her neck and breasts.

                    SHANA (CONT'D)
          Twenty bucks an hour.

Wayne makes eye contact with Shana, listening, deciding how much to pay them.

                    WAYNE
          The plants never lie.
              (eyeing Shana and Oscar)
          Let's see what the body count is in
          four hours. If you're fast,
          twenty. If not, it's fifteen.

Oscar and Shana take out their scissors.

Wayne pauses, noticing.

                    WAYNE (CONT'D)
          Brought your hardware. I like
          dat'.

Wayne exits the room through a half-broken door.

                    WAYNE (CONT'D)
          Olive oil and alcohol are on the
          table.

How to Kill a Bad Man

Wayne pops his head back in.

                WAYNE (CONT'D)
    And clock out for breaks.

Wayne disappears behind the door as they clean their scissors.

Wayne reappears, popping his head through the door.

                WAYNE (CONT'D)
    If any cars pull up, lemme' know.

                OSCAR
    More trimmers?

Wayne smiles, staring down Oscar.

                WAYNE
    Jus' lemme' know.

Wayne disappears behind the door.

INT. GROW SHACK HALLWAY - CONTINUOUS

Wayne walks through a hallway with small pot plants under fluorescent lights.

He disappears through another door.

INT. GROW SHACK FLOWERING ROOM - CONTINUOUS

Wayne scans the room full of mature pot plants, taking a deep breath. Overwhelmed.

He takes out the vial of coke, taking a couple efficient bumps off his hand.

He fills with energy, putting on a large pair of sunglasses designed for Antarctic expeditions.

He picks up a pair of gardening shears, cuts down a plant.

Josh Hyde

INT. GROW SHACK TRIM ROOM - CONTINUOUS

Wayne drops a huge pile of branches on the table, smiling.

                    WAYNE
          Here's a couple pounds.

Wayne picks up Shana's scissors from the table.

He picks up a bud, trimming it.

                    WAYNE (CONT'D)
          Unlike the dispensaries, I don't
          shave the buds. I don't do it and
          I don't pay you to do it.

The scissors are wild and uncontrolled, frantic at best.

                    WAYNE (CONT'D)
          Jus' leave it be if it has
          crystals. The main thing is don't
          spend too much time on each one.
                    (trimming)
          I'm savin' to buy a machine.

Wayne holds up the finished bud.

                    WAYNE (CONT'D)
          Voila...Got any questions Mr.
          Vowel? Guns?

Shana and Oscar shrug, "Nope."

                    WAYNE (CONT'D)
          Keep'em on the stem. And put'em on
          hangers.

Wayne sets the scissors down to put them on a hanger.

                    OSCAR
          You got a stereo?

                    WAYNE
          Yeah.
                    (pointing out the stereo)
          I'm cool with anythin', but monkey
          music.

How to Kill a Bad Man

Wayne winks at Shana and Oscar, disappearing.

Oscar pulls out his phone, queuing up some music. He presses play unleashing a soulful song, reminiscent of a Sergio Leone western.

Oscar and Shana look at each other, taking a deep breath.

Ready.

They remove the large branches from the main stalk, cutting the branches 10 inches or less.

A hand snaps off all of the large fan leaves.

Scissor blades cut off the tips of small leaves growing out of the buds.

The blades move from the bottom to the top. Shaping.

Fingers spin branches. Leaves fall off. The bud emerges.

They put the finished branches on hangers.

The scissors continue cutting. Leaves fall, piling up on the table.

                                                FLASHBACK TO.

INT. BASEMENT TRIM TABLE - EARLY MORNING

Early morning sunlight peaks in a small window. The basement is unfinished with bare concrete walls and floors.

A pile of trimmed buds sit on a circular table, lit with one desk lamp.

Shana looks at a table full of trimmed pot. Yawning.

A SKINNY GROWER enters carrying a pan of untrimmed pot.

                SKINNY GROWER
    This is it.

He empties the untrimmed buds on the table and fills the pan

Josh Hyde

with trimmed pot. He sets the pan on the table.

Shana and Oscar are tired, looking at the final pile.

          SKINNY GROWER (CONT'D)
         How many hours today? Including this?

Shana and Oscar look at each other.

          SKINNY GROWER (CONT'D)
         You're fast, that'll take you an hour.

               SHANA
         No way, that's a 2 hour pile. Maybe three. The weed is "larfy."

Shana holds up a stem, revealing tiny buds covered with an absurd amount of leaves.

             SHANA (CONT'D)
         See homie...Larfy.

The Skinny Grower nods, agreeing.

             SHANA (CONT'D)
         12 hours plus 2 hours for this pile.

               OSCAR
         14 hours times 20.
            (doing the math)
         That's $280 each.

The Skinny Grower takes out his cell phone, doing the math on his calculator app.

               SHANA
         $560 for both of us.

             SKINNY GROWER
         It took 14 hours cause you were goofing off. 20 an hour is for serious work. 15 is the rate for goofing off.

How to Kill a Bad Man

Shana and Oscar look at each other, annoyed.

> SHANA
> You just said how fast we are. And you didn't pick up the scissors once.

> SKINNY GROWER
> I had to take the plants down.

Shana and Oscar look at each other, rolling their eyes, "Whatever."

> OSCAR
> Seriously.

> SHANA
> It takes 3 minutes to take a plant down.
> (staring the Skinny Grower down)
> Look homie, it's 20 an hour.

The Skinny Grower shakes his head, "No."

> SKINNY GROWER
> 15 or nothing. It's your decision.

Shana and Oscar look at each other, accepting their fate.

> OSCAR
> (doing the math)
> It's $420.

> SHANA
> Can you throw in some herb?

The Skinny Grower smiles, nodding, "Yes." He counts out $410 from a wad of cash, putting it on the table.

Shana picks up the money, counting it out.

> SHANA (CONT'D)
> This is short 10 bucks.

> SKINNY GROWER
> I didn't have change. I'll hook you up fat.

                    OSCAR
            No worries. I got change.

Oscar takes out a $10, handing it to the Skinny Grower.

The Skinny Grower takes out a $20, exchanging bills.

                    SHANA
            $420 exactly.

The Skinny Grower sits down, resting.

                SKINNY GROWER
              (yawing)
            Let's get you some weed.

The Skinny Grower stands up, exiting the room. Oscar follows him.

                 OSCAR (O.S.)
            Can I have some water?

              SKINNY GROWER (O.S.)
            Follow me, champ.

Shana looks around, making sure she's alone.

She looks at the pan of trimmed weed.

She quickly opens her bag, taking out a large freezer ziplock bag.

Shana stuffs handfuls of trimmed weed into it. She closes the ziplock, hiding it in her bag.

She hears Oscar and the Skinny Grower returning.

Shana picks up her scissors, trimming a fresh branch.

Oscar and the Skinny Grower return with two glasses of water.

Oscar holds up a plastic sandwich bag, carelessly stuffed with old weed scraps.

                    OSCAR
              (faking a smile)
            Check it out.

Shana laughs to herself.

EXT. LARGE HOUSE WITH A HUGE YARD - EARLY MORNING

Shana and Oscar exit the front door of a large single-story house with a modern landscaped yard.

They absorb the morning, yawning. Sprinklers water the lawns.

> SHANA
> I need a pillow.

Oscar puts his arm around Shana as she snuggles into his chest tired.

> OSCAR
> I need a chauffeur.

Shana and Oscar get in the van, driving away. The sun is rising.

EXT. OSCAR'S DRIVEWAY - MORNING

Shana's hand is in soft focus against the sky. The colors smear together.

> SHANA
> The soft colors are back.

Oscar and Shana stand in the driveway, stretching.

She waives her hand in front of her eyes.

> SHANA (CONT'D)
> Come on focus. You can do it.

Her hands are out of focus, slowly becoming sharp.

They walk into Oscar's house.

Josh Hyde

INT. OSCAR'S HOUSE - LATE AFTERNOON

Oscar and Shana count out the money, annoyed.

                    OSCAR
$210.

Oscar hands her the extra $20. Shana doesn't take it, nodding, "Keep it."

                    SHANA
It's for gas and the set of tires I keep promising you.

Oscar smiles, keeping the extra money.

                    SHANA (CONT'D)
Just because homie lied and gave us shitty weed, doesn't mean we have to be shady.

Shana holds up the skimpy bag of weed.

                    SHANA (CONT'D)
And smoke garbage.

She tosses it into a trash can like a basketball into a hoop.

                    SHANA (CONT'D)
I got a surprise.

She looks at Oscar as a romantic moment grows.

He's timid. Unsure. Attracted.

                    OSCAR
I hate surprises.

Shana smiles, reaching into her bag. She pulls out the ziplock bag of stolen weed.

Oscar looks at the bag of weed. Relieved. Confused.

He grabs the bag, opening it up, smelling it.

                    OSCAR (CONT'D)
Is this...?

Shana smiles, "Yep."

> SHANA
> We just gotta' dry and cure it.
> You want half?

> OSCAR
> How much is here?

> SHANA
> A pound, maybe.

Oscar thinks about it, slowly nodding, "Yeah."

> SHANA (O.S.) (CONT'D)
> O, we need more weed.

END FLASHBACK.

INT. WAYNE'S TRIM ROOM - DAY

Shana nods her head at Oscar.

> SHANA
> O, we need more weed.

Her scissors keep working as Oscar notices the empty table.

> SHANA (CONT'D)
> Remember, you got to protect me
> from the Cali weirdos.

Oscar smiles, putting his finished bud on a hanger.

> SHANA (CONT'D)
> Practice on Wayne.

> OSCAR
> (exiting the room)
> No worries, my fearless leader.

INT. GROW SHACK BACK ROOM - DAY

Oscar wanders through a back room. Fluorescent lights hang from the ceiling.

Smaller pot plants grow under the lights. Oscar disappears through a doorway.

INT. GROW SHACK BACK ROOM WITH TOOLS - DAY

Oscar walks into a back room with tools lining the walls: pickaxes, posthole diggers, shovels, and stakes.

To the left, is an empty large blue plastic kiddie pool about 6 feet in diameter. A couple bags of soil are in it.

To the right, is a closed door with pink light glowing through the cracks.

                    OSCAR
Wayne?

Oscar waits for an answer. Silence.

                  OSCAR (CONT'D)
    (louder)
Wayne?

Silence.

                  OSCAR (CONT'D)
    (calling out)
Hey Wayne...We need more weed.

The door opens, BREAKING the silence. Wayne pops out, wearing blizzard proof sunglasses.

Fans BLOW a gust of air out of the room.

Oscar looks past Wayne. Curious.

                  WAYNE
    (blocking Oscar's view)
What up, O?

                    OSCAR
            We need more plants.

Wayne nods, "No problem," shutting the door. Silence.

The door SNAPS open as Wayne pops out.

                    WAYNE
            Just knock on the door next time...
                (knocking on the door)
            And I'll bring out more ladies.

The door SLAMS. Silence.

The door SNAPS opens. Wayne pops out.

                    WAYNE (CONT'D)
            Any cars?

Oscar nods, "No."

                    WAYNE (CONT'D)
            Jus' lemme know.

The door SLAMS. Silence.

INT. GROW SHACK FLOWERING ROOM - DAY

The garden is half empty. Wayne pulls out the coke, taking a couple more bumps for energy. He SNORTS, clearing his nose.

Wayne scans the room.

                    WAYNE
                (pointing at empty pots)
            1...4, 5, 6...9,13, 14...18, 19...

Wayne smiles at the progress.

He picks up a pair of garden sheers, selecting a small plant, cutting off the branches.

                    WAYNE (CONT'D)
            Twenty.

Josh Hyde

INT. WAYNE'S TRIM ROOM - DAY

Wayne sets a few branches on the table.

          WAYNE
A couple stragglers.

Wayne looks at the full hangers, SNIFFLING, feeling the coke.

          WAYNE (CONT'D)
   (drinking a beer)
Ya'll wanna' a break?

          SHANA
How long we been working?

          WAYNE
'Bout 5 hours.

Shana and Oscar look at each other, deciding to take a break.

          WAYNE (CONT'D)
At this rate we'll finish in 7, maybe 8 hours.

Shana and Oscar put down their scissors, standing to stretch their legs.

          OSCAR
Not bad.

Oscar takes out his phone, reading the time.

          OSCAR (CONT'D)
5 hours even.

Shana stretches her arms over her head, revealing a tight stomach and cute hips.

          SHANA
That feels like 5 hours.

Wayne checks out her tight body, eventually finding her face.

          WAYNE
Ya'll gotta' go to the bathroom or anythin'?

How to Kill a Bad Man

Oscar and Shana nod, "Yes."

                    WAYNE (CONT'D)
   It's all in the house.

Wayne points to the house.

                    WAYNE (CONT'D)
   I need a beer. I'll see ya'll
   inside.

Wayne shuffles out as Oscar and Shana clean their scissors.

                    SHANA
   I can clean up.

Oscar nods agreeing.

                    SHANA (CONT'D)
    (winking at Oscar,
    whispering)
   Keep an eye on the creeper.

Oscar smiles, walking to the house.

Alone. Shana pushes piles of leaves into a 5 gallon bucket.

She takes a ziplock freezer bag out of her pocket. She stuffs trimmed buds into it until it's full.

She seals it, putting the freezer bag into her shoulder bag.

EXT. WAYNE'S HOME - DAY

Wayne and Oscar stand in the house, looking at the design.

It's filled with nice things, the opposite of Wayne.

                    WAYNE
   Ya'll just crushed it for 5 hours
   with no break.

                    OSCAR
   Nice place.

                        WAYNE
            That's some all-star team shit,
            right ther'.

Shana joins them. She's smoking a bowl, passing it to Oscar.

Wayne watches. Attracted.

                        WAYNE (CONT'D)
            Ya'll married?

Shana and Oscar look at each, feeling awkward.

                        SHANA
            Just friends.

                        OSCAR
            It's easier that way.

                        WAYNE
                (eyeing Shana)
            So I got a chance.

Wayne smiles, revealing his brown teeth, laughing to fill the awkward silence.

                        WAYNE (CONT'D)
            Bathroom's over ther'.
                (pointing out the door)
            Food and beer's in the fridge.

                        OSCAR
            Thanks.

Oscar disappears into the bathroom, handing the bowl to Wayne.

Wayne takes a hit, passing it to Shana.

                        SHANA
            No thanks.

Wayne eyes Shana as she ignores him.

He takes another hit, openly staring at her legs and breasts.

She notices him, "100% creeper."

> WAYNE
> You lik' my house?

Shana fakes a smile, nodding, "Yeah."

> WAYNE (CONT'D)
> It's a geo-desic-dome. Y'ever seen
> one? A guy named Bucky built'em.
> They call'em Bucky balls.

Wayne laughs at his joke as Shana pretends to look at the house.

> WAYNE (CONT'D)
> Been up here for 15 years. It's
> nice n'quiet.

He takes a hit from the bowl, blowing the smoke at Shana.

> WAYNE (CONT'D)
> I jus' hang out and grow. Chill
> with m'lady friends. Y'ever been
> with a grower?

Wayne offers her the bowl.

Shana's eyes focus on Wayne, shaking her head, "No."

> WAYNE (CONT'D)
> You can smoke all you want. Go to
> whatever shows you want.
>   (staring her down)
> Jus' enjoy life.

Wayne winks, smiling. He offers Shana the bowl, again.

> SHANA
> My life is pretty enjoyable.

> WAYNE
> It could be very enjoyable. I can
> take care of you.

Shana looks at the bathroom door, ignoring the pick up lines.

                    WAYNE (CONT'D)
          Jus' chill and go to shows. Crash
          out up here...The Bucky ball.
                (smiling)
          Nothin' serious.

He looks at her like a piece of meat.

                    WAYNE (CONT'D)
          Jus' fun.

She ignores Wayne as he gets closer, slowly invading her
personal space.

                    WAYNE (CONT'D)
          You like to dance?

Shana looks at him. Intimidated. He gets closer, swaying
his body, attempting to dance with her.

                                        FLASHBACK TO.

INT. CONCERT/DANCE FLOOR - NIGHT

Darkness. Flashing beams of colored light illuminate a sea
of hands.

Andrew, Lucy, Shana, Oscar, Click and Clack dance to ethereal
dub-step fused with trip-hop.

Click's body gyrates with the beat as his feet, knees, and
waist execute break dancing moves. Clack is robot dancing.

Shana and Oscar dance together. Getting close.

                    SHANA
          Last chance.

Shana puts her arms around Oscar.

                    OSCAR
                (smiling)
          Isn't it an all women farm?

Oscar puts his hands around her waist, slow dancing.

SHANA
(nodding, yes)
You're kind of like a woman trapped in a man's body.

Oscar looks at Shana, unsure.

OSCAR
I was gonna' stay at the dispensary, maybe get a raise.

SHANA
You need money, right?

Oscar nods, "Yeah."

OSCAR
I need a regular paycheck. Not Cali rednecks, police raids, and trim fairies.

Shana nods, agreeing with him.

SHANA
That's why I need you. To keep the creepers away.

Oscar smiles as they dance, getting closer.

SHANA (CONT'D)
And help drive.

OSCAR
I'm great with creepers.

Beams of light flash by them as darkness consumes the dance floor.

EXT. MOUNTAIN OVERLOOK TRAIL - NIGHT

On the horizon, a small city lights up the night.

Oscar and Shana come into focus, sitting on a cliff.

Their eyes flirt with each other, wanting to share a kiss.

Shana notices flashlight beams in the darkness, interrupting the moment.

> SHANA
> (shouting)
> Just walk toward the mountain.

Shana and Oscar watch the beams stumbling through the night.

> ANDREW
> (Southern accent,
> shouting)
> Where are y'all?

> LUCY
> (yelling)
> If I get eaten by a bear, my ghost is gonna' be pissed.

Confused flashlight beams point in all directions, searching.

> CLACK
> (shouting)
> I just want to smoke weed.

Shana and Oscar sit on the rocks, watching. The moment is gone.

> CLICK
> (shouting)
> I didn't agree to cardiovascular activity, darkness,...
> (taking a deep breath,
> yelling)
> And bears.

Two flashlight beams point at each other.

> CLACK
> Click, I see you.

The beams of light move toward each other.

> CLICK
> (yelling)
> Don't smoke the hash without me.

All the flashlights are together, marching in a uniform line, approaching the cliff.

Click, Clack, Andrew, and Lucy emerge from the forest trail into the moonlight.

>CLACK
>(raising his hands to the sky)
>Hello mother nature.
>(inhaling deeply)
>I'm home.

Oscar and Shana shine flashlights on their comrades from the cliff above the trail.

Lucy, Andrew, Click and Clack look up, finding Oscar and Shana.

Clack waives, "Hello."

END FLASHBACK.

INT. WAYNE'S HOUSE - DAY

Oscar exits the bathroom, interrupting Wayne dancing towards Shana.

Wayne shifts away from her. Guilty.

She walks past Oscar into the bathroom. Annoyed.

Oscar walks to the kitchen, finding a bag of chips. Oblivious.

>OSCAR
>These fair game?

Wayne nods, "Go for it."

Oscar munches on the chips, watching Wayne take out the vial of coke. He SNIFFS some off his hand.

He notices Oscar.

                        WAYNE
            You wan' some fuel?

Wayne offers Oscar the vial.

                        OSCAR
            I'm good with the chips.

                        WAYNE
            Ready to get back to work?

Oscar nods, "Yeah."

                        WAYNE (CONT'D)
            I'll meet you back up ther'.
                (smiling)
            Too much beer.

                        OSCAR
            Sounds good, boss.

Oscar leaves the house with the bag of chips.

Wayne watches Oscar walk to the grow shack.

Alone.

INT. BATHROOM - DAY

Shana sits on the toilet, taking a piss. She shakes her head, disgusted.

She takes out her cell phone, quickly typing a text, "O, he's gettin' weird. Wait for me. PRACTICE IS OVER :-("

Shana sends the text, putting the phone in her pocket.

She grabs a wad of toilet paper; wiping, flushing, and buttoning up her pants. Annoyed.

The phone VIBRATES a new message.

She takes the phone out, reading, "You are out of the service area. All messages will be delivered when you return to the service area."

How to Kill a Bad Man

                    SHANA
        (talking to herself)
   Shit.

She takes out the bonsai scissors, looking at the blades.

INT. WAYNE'S HOUSE - DAY

Wayne SNORTS some coke off his hand, feeling good.

Shana comes out of the bathroom, scanning the room for Oscar.

She's alone with Wayne.

He reaches into his pocket, pulling out a wad of hundred dollar bills.

He slowly peels off $100, holding it out.

                    WAYNE
   Here's the money for trimmin'.

He peels off another $400, putting it with the $100.

Shana eyes the money. Uncomfortable.

                    WAYNE (CONT'D)
   For the gun show.

Wayne holds up his arm, flexing, imitating Shana.

He counts out another $600, adding it to the wad.

                    WAYNE (CONT'D)
        (looking at her breasts)
   Let's keep the show goin'.

Shana stares him down, emotionless. Unimpressed.

                    SHANA
   I'm not a grow ho.

Wayne slowly nods, "Okay."

                    WAYNE
   And if you don't want the extra

cash...That's fine. I understand.

He puts the $1,000 down and holds out a $100 bill.

>   WAYNE (CONT'D)
>   For trimmin'.

Shana takes the $100 bill as Wayne grabs her, bear hugging her skinny body.

>   WAYNE (CONT'D)
>   Shhhhhh. Shhhhh. It's fine.
>   (tightly squeezing her)
>   I'll pay for the whole show.

Wayne gropes her crotch and breasts as she STRUGGLES.

Shana reaches for the scissors, hanging out of her back pocket.

Wayne grabs her arms, trapping them.

>   WAYNE (CONT'D)
>   Shhhh, it'll be a quick show.

His hands snake around her waste, finding the buttons to her pants, pinning her against the wall.

He unbuttons her pants, shoving his hand in, forcing his fingers into her.

She YELLS as Wayne let's go of her wrist to cover her mouth.

Shana slowly reaches for the scissors, again.

She takes a deep breath, pulling them out.

Wayne's hand is lost in her pants as Shana stabs his forearm, running the blade down to his wrist.

Blood pours out of the large wound as Wayne grabs his arm, stepping back.

He looks at the blood-covered arm, calmly surprised.

>   SHANA
>   (yelling)
>   Just give me the money.

He looks up at Shana, exploding with a a back hand SLAP, sending her across the room.

> WAYNE
> Shhhiiiiit. We're way past dat'.

Shana picks herself up as the scissors dangle from her hands.

Wayne snatches a wooden stool, whipping it at her, SMASHING Shana to the ground. Barely conscious.

The bonsai scissors, dripping with blood.

The wooden stool in pieces.

Shana is lying on the ground, unable to get up.

Wayne closes in, blood dripping from his arm. He kicks her hard.

She GASPS breathless.

Wayne straddles her, grabbing her face with his good hand.

> WAYNE (CONT'D)
> The show must go on.

Wayne unbuckles his belt as Shana's fingers find a piece of the stool.

She grabs it, swinging it at his head.

He blocks it, grabbing her arm, staring her down.

Shana's free hand jams the bonsai scissors into his ear.

> WAYNE (CONT'D)
> Fuck!

Wayne rolls off Shana with the scissors sticking out of his ear. The pain snaps Wayne to his feet.

> WAYNE (CONT'D)
> You're dead...I'm gonna'...

He touches the scissors, carefully trying to pull them out.

The scissors are stuck.

Blood soaks his shirt from the neck down.

Shana curls up, grabbing the stool leg, protecting herself.

>   WAYNE (CONT'D)
> I'm gonn'...I'm...

He clumsily steps toward Shana, stopping. Unable to move.

>   WAYNE (CONT'D)
>   (mumbling)
> Stupid...grow ho.

He tries to take another step, frozen in place. He collapses in front of Shana.

DEAD.

The house is SILENT.

Shana BREATHES heavy, staring at Wayne's still body.

She slowly picks herself up, covered in blood. Trembling.

>   FLASHBACK TO.

INT. DISPENSARY TRIM TABLE - DAY

TREE, 28, an LSD and Molly-crazed trimmer with dreadlocks and a beard, MUMBLES to himself as he sits in a chair. He's wearing a flat-brimmed hat and baggy clothes.

A visitor badge hangs around his neck. He dances as he sits, sweating profusely.

Martin, Andrew, Lucy, Shana, Oscar, Click and Clack sit around the table trimming.

>   TREE
>   (talking to himself)
> And then I was dancing...In the
> light...

How to Kill a Bad Man

The trimmers stop working to watch Tree talk to himself.

Stealthily, the group rolls their chairs away from him.

Distancing themselves from cray cray. Crazy.

Martin rubs both hands in circles on the table, collecting scissor hash. He slowly rolls his chair away from the table.

Tree's eyes are closed. His body is still, dancing in his mind.

>   TREE (CONT'D)
> But my friends weren't there. I
> was lost, but I wasn't. I was one.
> One.

Shana and Oscar are the only ones left at the table with Tree.

Lucy, Martin, Andrew, Click and Clack are watching, safely orbiting the table.

>   CLICK
>   (whispering)
> Homie's trippin.

Click nods his head at Tree.

>   TREE
>   (dancing in the chair)
> One...One...One...

>   CLICK
>   (whispering)
> And rolling.

Shana watches Tree, disturbed. She makes eye contact with Oscar, "This dude is losing his shit."

Shana nods, "Can you deal with him?"

Oscar shakes his head quickly, "Hell, no."

>   SHANA
>   (whispering)
> I'm small. He's big.

She motions with her arms, "Look at how big he is."

                  SHANA (CONT'D)
        (whispering)
    He's got acid strength.

                  OSCAR
        (whispering)
    You got Mexican strength.

Shana pleads with her eyes, "Seriously."

                  SHANA
    I'm only half Mexican...
        (begging with her eyes)
    Please.

Oscar accepts his fate, protecting Shana.

He rolls his chair closer to Tree as Shana distances herself.

                  OSCAR
    Hey, Tree.
        (pausing)
    How you doin' buddy?

Tree's body is still as his eyes look around, hallucinating.

Oscar looks at Click and Clack for support.

They shake their heads, "Don't do it."

                  CLICK
    I don't want to die today. I'm 22.

Clack waives his hand, trying to get Tree's attention.

Nothing.

                  CLACK
    Bro...Roll away slowly and forget
    Tree.

Clack shakes his head, "Not today."

                  CLICK
    Tree doesn't exist right now.

Clack points at Martin.

                    MARTIN
      I got two kids...A wife that hates
      me...
          (staring at Oscar)
      I'm just here for the scissor hash.

Martin nods his head, "Don't do it, dude."

                    ANDREW
          (Southern accent)
      Tree is gone, man. No one's home.

Clack waives both hands to get Tree's attention as Lucy slaps his arms down.

                    LUCY
          (whispering)
      Are you cray cray Texas?

Clack nods, "Yes," slowly realizing he doesn't want to be crazy he nods, "No."

                    LUCY (CONT'D)
          (turning to Oscar)
      We don't need any heroes.

Oscar turns to Shana, "What now?"

Shana's eyes point to Tree.

Oscar takes a deep breath, centering himself.

                    OSCAR
      What up, Tree?

Tree intensely focuses on Oscar with full-blown acid-vision.

Everyone scatters from the chairs, hiding under the table.

Oscar's aura is glowing as sparks fly out.

                    OSCAR (CONT'D)
      How about a 10 minute break, buddy?

Tree's eyes are overwhelmed by Oscar's aura.

                    TREE
          You're glowing.

                    OSCAR
          That's cool. I always glow when
          it's time for a break.

Oscar gets up from his chair, escorting Tree away from the table.

Tree GIGGLES to himself.

He looks at Oscar, acid-vision. Oscar's aura is radiating colors.

                    TREE
          You're my friend...Oscar...
               (reaching to touch Oscar's
               face)
          ...Oscar...
               (whispering)
          Are we in the spirit world?

Oscar leads Tree through a door.

                    OSCAR
               (pausing)
          Yes and no...

EXT. PARKING LOT - DAY

Tree and Oscar walk through the parking lot.

                    TREE
          Why does the spirit world look like
          a parking lot?

Oscar points out a bike.

                    OSCAR
          Is that your bike?

                    TREE
          How did she get here?

Tree looks at Oscar, confused.

> TREE (CONT'D)
> We got to take her with us. She
> doesn't like the spirit world.

Oscar nods, agreeing.

Tree smiles, helpless, as Oscar loads him into the van like a child.

Oscar opens the trunk, loading up the bike.

> TREE (O.S.) (CONT'D)
> (whispering)
> Oooscar.

Oscar stops, looking around. Listening.

> TREE (O.S.) (CONT'D)
> (whispering)
> Osccaaaaar.

He closes the trunk, revealing Tree hiding against the van, staring him down.

> TREE (CONT'D)
> (whispering)
> Oooossscar. I'm over here. Shhh.

Oscar smiles, uncomfortable and scared.

> TREE (CONT'D)
> The white buffalo wants me to watch
> over you.

> OSCAR
> White Buffalo?

Tree is silent, staring at the white minivan. He touches it, slowly nodding his head, "This white buffalo."

> TREE
> Tatonka.

Oscar loads Tree into the front passenger seat.

He puts the seat belt on him, closing the door.

>   TREE (CONT'D)
>   (chanting)
>   Tatonka...Tatonka...Tatonka...

Oscar walks to the driver side, looking back at the warehouse.

Shana is standing by the warehouse door, smiling, "Thanks."

Oscar waives, "Bye."

>   TREE (CONT'D)
>   (chanting)
>   Tatonka...Tatonka...

The van pulls away.

>   OSCAR (O.S.)
>   Shana...Where's Wayne?...Shana.

                                             FLASHBACK END.

INT. WAYNE'S HOUSE - DAY

Shana stares at the floor. Trembling.

>   OSCAR
>   Where's Wayne?

Oscar enters the front door.

>   OSCAR (CONT'D)
>   I need more weed.

Her eyes are fixed on the floor. The couch covers what she's looking at.

She turns, looking at Oscar. Bloody. Broken. Scratched up.

She nods, "No."

Shana shifts her eyes, focusing on something behind the couch. Trembling.

How to Kill a Bad Man

Oscar stops, finding Wayne's bloody body. Scissors sticking out of his head.

He closes his mouth, inhaling through his nose, smelling death.

He puts the neck of his t-shirt over his nose, turning to Shana.

>   SHANA
> He tried to...and I...
>   (stabbing with trembling hands)
> He wouldn't stop...I tried...

Shana buries her head between her arms. Relieved and broken.

>   SHANA (CONT'D)
> Where were you?

Shana stares down Oscar.

Oscar doesn't have an answer.

>   SHANA (CONT'D)
> Why didn't you wait?

Oscar is quiet, turning away from Shana, looking at the body.

>   OSCAR
> We got to call the cops.

Shana is scared, shaking her head "No."

>   SHANA
> We can't.

>   OSCAR
> It was self-defense.

>   SHANA
> We're on a weed farm. He probably
> hasn't paid taxes in 10 years.

>   OSCAR
> We came to work and he...tried
> to...to...attack you.
>   (looking at Shana)

And you killed him in self-defense.

Shana trembles, shaking her head, "No."

                    SHANA
Let's just leave.

Oscar looks at her, "Are you crazy?"

                SHANA (CONT'D)
Fuck him.

                   OSCAR
It's gonna' look like we murdered him.

A pause grows.

                OSCAR (CONT'D)
What if Click and Clack call this homie? Or if the people he was waiting on show up?

                    SHANA
We can't call the cops.

Shana stares down Oscar, vulnerable. Shana slowly shakes her head, "No cops."

                SHANA (CONT'D)
   (trembling)
No cops.

Oscar looks at Shana, thinking of what to do.

                   OSCAR
No cops.

Oscar kneels down by the body. He's wearing rubber gloves from trimming.

His hands search through Wayne's pocket, pulling out a wad of money, vial of coke, and a cell phone.

Shana looks at the vial of coke as Oscar pockets all of the belongings.

How to Kill a Bad Man

Oscar makes eye contact with Shana, "What do we do now?"

An awkward pause grows as they look at the body, thinking.

> OSCAR (CONT'D)
> We have to chop him up.

Oscar scans the pool of blood.

> OSCAR (CONT'D)
> And clean up this mess.

> SHANA
> That's way past self-defense.

Oscar tries to lift the body, but can't. It's too heavy.

> OSCAR
> It's the only way to bury him.

Oscar and Shana look at each other, "It's the only way."

INT. GROW SHACK - DAY

An axe leans against a wall.

EXT. SIDE OF HOUSE - CONTINUOUS

A wood chopping block is surrounded by piles of firewood.

EXT. HOUSE - CONTINUOUS

The body is in the middle of a tarp. Shana holds one side as Oscar holds the other, carrying the body to the grow shack.

Oscar sets his side down.

> SHANA
> What are you doing?

> OSCAR
> I gotta rest.

                    SHANA
          Come on.

Oscar picks up his end of the tarp, taking a deep breath.

They carry the body into the grow shack.

In the background a UFO floats across the horizon, disappearing.

INT. GROW SHACK/BACK ROOM - CONTINUOUS

The wood chopping block is in the middle of the large circular blue plastic kiddie pool. Soil lines the bottom.

Shana and Oscar set down the body next to the pool. Resting.

                    OSCAR
          On three.

Oscar and Shana pick up the tarp, rocking the body back and forth.

                    SHANA
          One...Two...Three.

They release the body as it flops into the pool. Lifeless.

Oscar pulls the tarp from under the body and folds it up.

Shana and Oscar look at each other. Exhausted.

They sit down.

Shana eyes the axe.

Oscar catches his breath. He pulls out the vial of coke, holding it up.

Shana's eyes find the vial.

Their eyes meet, "It's the only way."

Oscar SNORTS some off his hand as Shana INHALES a big line.

There is more left in the vial. They look at each other, deciding to save it for later.

Alert. Ready. Oscar picks up the axe as the corners of his mouth jitter in circles.

> OSCAR
> I think an arm or a leg is the way to go.

Shana looks at the body, immediately agreeing.

> SHANA
> I'm down with arms and legs.

Oscar and Shana adjust the body, putting the arm on the chopping block.

> OSCAR
> It's like cutting up a chicken.

Shana pulls out her phone.

> SHANA
> I never cut up a chicken before. I usually buy it in pieces.

> OSCAR
> I went through a cooking phase. You got to cut the wings or thighs off first.

Shana types, "Cut up, whole chicken" on her phone. The phone isn't getting a signal.

> SHANA
> Give me your phone.

Oscar gives Shana his cell phone.

His phone has one bar. Shana smiles, typing in "Cut up, whole chicken." Buffering.

> SHANA (CONT'D)
> Here's one.

Shana and Oscar watch the video.

Oscar practices his axe swing while watching.

                    VIDEO NARRATOR
          The first step to de-boning a
          chicken is to cut off the legs.

They line up Wayne's leg.

                    VIDEO NARRATOR (CONT'D)
          Make sure to cut in between the
          bones for the best results.

Oscar raises the axe over his head, taking a deep breath.

Wayne's leg shifts out of position as he COUGHS himself awake, slowly opening his bloody eyes.

                    WAYNE
             (mumbling)
          I'm gonna' kill y'all.

Shana and Oscar step back taking a defensive position, "Fuck."

Wayne GRUNTS, STRUGGLING, weakly moving his legs.

He carefully grabs the scissors, sticking out of his ear, unable to pull them out.

                    WAYNE (CONT'D)
             (mumbling)
          Motherf...mmmme...

They watch Wayne, helpless in the pool. Oscar lets go of the axe as it falls to the floor.

                    OSCAR
          I can't.

                    SHANA
          We can't just stop. We got the
          axe, the video...We almost got the
          leg.

Oscar is quiet, sitting down.

                    WAYNE
             (softly)
          Take me...Hospital.

> OSCAR
> Let's take him to the hospital.

> SHANA
> Fuck the hospital. O, look at me.

Shana grabs his face, making Oscar look at her.

Shana's face is scratched and bruised.

> SHANA (CONT'D)
> He...
> (trembling)
> Needs to die.

Oscar nods, "No."

> SHANA (CONT'D)
> And what do we say?

> OSCAR
> We found him wandering in the mountains after a bear attacked him.
> (staring her down)
> Say whatever you want. I'm not a killer.

> WAYNE
> Hospital.

Shana is quiet, picking up the axe, staring at Wayne. Thinking.

> SHANA
> He's not going anywhere.

She slowly positions herself over his body.

Shana grabs the scissors as Wayne SCREAMS from the pain.

> SHANA (CONT'D)
> And I want my scissors back.

Shana pulls the scissors out of his ear.

Blood spurts out of his head, slowly losing pressure.

Wayne SCREAMS, choking on the blood, losing consciousness.

Shana tests the scissors. They work; she's smiling.

INT. GROW SHACK/BACK ROOM - MOMENTS LATER

Oscar feels Wayne's wrist. No pulse.

>					OSCAR
> I think he's dead this time.

Oscar adjust the body, putting the leg on the chopping block.

Shana steps back, picking up the axe. The leg shifts out of position.

>					SHANA
>				(looking at Oscar)
>			You gotta' hold his leg.

Oscar grabs the leg.

Shana looks at Oscar, "I'm not ready." Shana steps back, taking a couple deep breaths.

She looks up at Oscar, he's holding up the vial of coke.

They INHALE the last of the coke as their jaws grind in circles, "Ready."

Shana raises the ax over her head.

She swings, slicing the thigh as blood spurts onto their faces.

Wayne's body is lifeless.

Shana and Oscar are frozen in place with their eyes closed, covered in blood.

>				SHANA (CONT'D)
>			That wasn't in the video.

                    OSCAR
            (wiping the blood off his face)
        Nope.

Shana opens her eyes, wiping the blood away.

She takes a couple slow practice swings as Oscar secures the leg.

                    OSCAR (CONT'D)
        You ready?

She raises the ax.

                    SHANA
        I'm ready.

                    OSCAR
        One...

                    SHANA
        Two..

                    SHANA AND OSCAR
        Three.

Shana swings, CHOPPING the leg off.

                                        FLASHBACK TO.

INT. DISPENSARY TRIM TABLE - DAY

Martin, Lucy, Andrew, Click, Clack, Oscar, and Shana trim at a large conference table.

RANDOM NEWBIE TRIMMERS fill the table.

                    MARTIN
        I'm just saying when the time comes
        you'll know. My father was a
        Jewish colonel in the German Army
        and when Hitler came to power, he
        was still loyal to the Nazis.

Oscar listens along with Lucy, Andrew, Shana, Click and Clack.

MARTIN(CONT'D)
Then his buddies were like, "Hey man, we got to get you and your family out of here."

Martin finishes a bud, tossing it into an aluminum turkey pan.

MARTIN (CONT'D)
That's how the Koenigsbergs survived. Having friends. If they didn't tell him to leave, I might not be here today.

OSCAR
Where'd he go?

MARTIN
(British accent)
London.

CLICK
(British accent)
There is no way, I'd kill any of you. Even if I was a Nazi and you were all Jews.

LUCY
Awe, that's sweet.

CLICK
(British accent)
But the new trimmers, I'd totally kill all of them for one of you guys.
 (whispering in a British
 accent)
They're not Jewish like us.

OSCAR
Don't kill the newbies.

CLICK
(British accent)
What if I just take off a leg?

How to Kill a Bad Man

Oscar and Shana make eye contact with Click, shaking their heads, "No."

> CLICK (CONT'D)
> A foot?

> SHANA
> Deep breaths, Click. Deep breaths.

Shana INHALES deeply looking at Click.

> SHANA (CONT'D)
> (exhaling)
> Ohmmmmm...and inhale
> (exhaling)
> Ohmmmmmm...

Click closes his eyes and chants to himself.

> CLICK
> Ohmmmmmmmm...

> MARTIN
> (joining in)
> Ohmmmmmmm...

> OSCAR
> Ohmmmmmmm...

> ANDREW
> (Southern Accent)
> Ohmmmmmmm.

The table gets quiet after the final, "Ohm."

All is calm. Serene.

Click is basking in the final glow of the "Ohmment," eyes closed.

> CLICK
> (opening his eyes)
> Yo, that Ohmment worked.
> (smiling)
> I'm mad calm now.

Click looks at the Newbie Trimmers. They're staring at the group of "Ohmers."

     CLICK (CONT'D)
 My ohmies rejoice in the flowers of
 life.

Click grabs a handful of untrimmed buds, dropping them in front of the Newbie Trimmers.

     ANDREW
 Ya'll ever feel like the slaves of
 this company?

No one answers. Shana smiles at Andrew.

     SHANA
 Don't worry. The machines are on
 the way.

Shana eyes the Newbie Trimmers. They're all slow.

     SHANA (CONT'D)
 Once the machines get here...

Shana nods her head in the direction of the Newbie Trimmers.

     SHANA (CONT'D)
  (whispering)
 They'll replace us with these
 scabs.

     CLACK
  (whispering)
 The visitors.

     SHANA
 I make $13.50.

Shana nods her head at Martin, "What do you make?"

     MARTIN
 $13 an hour.

Shana looks at Lucy.

How to Kill a Bad Man

> LUCY
> $13.75...

Shana turns to Andrew.

> ANDREW
> ...$13...

Shana settles on Oscar.

> OSCAR
> After taxes...$10 an hour.

> CLICK AND CLACK
> ...$13.50...

> SHANA
> We're already dead.

Shana finishes trimming a bud in her hand. She looks at it, tossing it in the aluminum turkey pan.

She picks up a large bud, trimming it.

> SHANA (CONT'D)
> I'm gonna' milk this as long as possible. Then go to Cali for some real cash. No taxes. No bullshit.
> (talking to herself)
> Get a house, blow it up, and harvest 30 pounds. Retire from trimming.

Shana tosses the finished bud in the aluminum turkey pan.

> SHANA (CONT'D)
> Maybe learn to make hash.

Martin, Andrew, Lucy, Oscar, Click and Clack get an idea, staring down Shana.

> SHANA (CONT'D)
> What?

Everyone is quiet, smiling.

                    OSCAR
            Why wait?

Martin rubs his hand on the table, showing his palm to Shana and Oscar.

                    MARTIN
            We have a lot of scissor hash.

Shana smiles at Martin.

                                    FLASHBACK END.

INT. GROW SHACK/BACK ROOM - DAY

Shana and Oscar stand over the kiddie pool, wearing rubber gloves. Bloody.

Oscar holds a garbage bag open as Shana picks up an arm, dropping it in.

Oscar ties up the bag.

He opens up a fresh garbage bag as Shana sticks both of Wayne's legs in.

EXT. VAN - CONTINUOUS

They put the various garbage bags in the van.

They count the wad of money from Wayne's pocket.

It's $2,200. Shana looks at the cash, nodding at Oscar, "Keep it."

                    SHANA
            It's for the tires I keep promising
            you.

Oscar smiles, pocketing the money.
EXT. SIDE OF HOUSE - DAY

A large pile of firewood is stacked by the house.

Oscar and Shana move the pile of firewood, uncovering fresh

dirt.

Oscar digs.

Shana drags the kiddie pool into position. It's filled with blood-soaked dirt.

Shana picks up a shovel, helping dig.

EXT. SIDE OF HOUSE - MOMENT LATER

The hole is ready. Shana and Oscar hold the sides of the kiddie pool, emptying the blood-soaked dirt into the hole.

EXT. SIDE OF HOUSE - MOMENT LATER

Clean water from a hose washes out the kiddie pool.

The blood drains into the hole.

INT. WAYNE'S HOUSE - DAY

A pool of blood dries on a tile floor.

Shana and Oscar stare at it.

Shana spreads soil on the blood, soaking it up.

They collect the blood soaked dirt in the kiddie pool.

EXT. SIDE OF HOUSE - MOMENTS LATER

Shana and Oliver tip over the kiddie pool, emptying the bloody dirt into the hole.

Oscar shovels clean dirt into the hole.

It's full.

Oscar and Shana re-stack the firewood on top of the filled-in hole.

                    OSCAR
          After you left, it was good for a
          couple months. Then the triminators
          showed up.

                    SHANA
          Did they find out about the hash
          oil?

Oscar smiles, "No."

                    OSCAR
          They're clueless. The machines
          make so much waste. Martin blows
          it into shatter and we sell it on
          Instagram.

                    SHANA
          You grew up Oscar. You're not that
          wide-eyed Midwest kid anymore.

Oscar continues stacking wood.

                    OSCAR
          How was last summer?

Shana gets quiet, picking up a piece of wood, adding it to
the pile.

                    SHANA
          Some summers are better than
          others.

Shana looks at him.

                                        FLASHBACK TO.

EXT. SMALL BLACK CAR - DUSK

The final rays of sunlight pierce the dark horizon as Shana
drives west.

She smiles. Free.

                    SHANA (V.O.)
          Our farm was good, but the one next

to ours messed it up.

EXT. POT FARM - DAY

An OLD HIPPIE with a long beard, 60's, and a YOUNG HIPPIE, 30's, drink beer as they stare blankly at a forest.

FLASHBACK END.

EXT. SIDE OF HOUSE - DAY

Shana pauses, holding a piece of firewood.

> SHANA
> Just a bunch of greedy cowboys and we got caught up.
> (looking at Oscar)
> The cops are cool if you're good to the land and the town, but if you're an ass...
> (nodding her head, slowly)
> The mountain is coming down on you.

Oscar listens.

FLASHBACK TO.

EXT. MOUTAIN SIDE - DAY

The Old Hippie drives a bulldozer, carving a clearing in a forest. The Young Hippie watches.

> SHANA (V.O.)
> These jokers took a bulldozer and flattened half their land. It was a huge scar on top of a hill. Fucking cowboys.

EXT. MOUNTAIN SIDE - DAY

From the air, the freshly bulldozed dirt scar contrasts the green forest.

The Old and Young hippie transplant pot plants into the field.

> SHANA (V.O.)
> It's Cali. People get cra cra.

EXT. SMALL COUNTY AIRPORT - DAY

Looking through binoculars, a SHERIFF watches the Old and Young hippie planting pot.

> SHANA (V.O.)
> The cops saw the clearing and
> started flying helicopters over the
> mountain.

The brown clearing can be seen from the airport.

> SHANA (V.O.)
> They waited until harvest, made us
> sweat it out all summer. As soon
> as the harvest started, it was on.

Helicopters descend from the sky as RANDOM HIPPIES scatter into the woods.

OFFICERS in swat team gear, guns, and machetes chop down and burn all the pot plants.

EXT. SHANA'S FARM - DAY

Shana walks through a pot field, tucked under rows of trees.

She picks off big fan leaves from pot plants.

> SHANA (V.O.)
> My lady had the in.

The Sheriff appears talking to JANE, 50's, an older hippie woman. They hug and Jane gives the Sheriff a stack of money.

> SHANA (V.O.)
> We harvested 500 plants early and
> had to take them to a whole other
> farm along with the trim crew.

How to Kill a Bad Man

EXT. POT FIELD - DAY

Shana harvests plants with groups of other workers.

They toss whole plants, the size of Christmas trees, into a beat up Mazda truck.

INT. OLD BARN - DUSK

Shana ties up one plant at a time to strings, hanging from the rafters.

>SHANA (V.O.)
>I lived in a tent the rest of the summer.

EXT. FIELD FULL OF TENTS - DUSK

Eight tents are scattered through a field. Shana walks to her tent, getting in.

INT. TENT - DUSK

Shana smokes a bowl, laying in her tent. Dirty. Tired. Alone.

>SHANA (V.O.)
>I made some money, but not enough to start my grow.

>FLASHBACK END.

EXT. SIDE OF HOUSE - DAY

Shana and Oscar stack the last pieces of wood on the pile.

>SHANA
>You're lucky you didn't come.

Oscar listens, remembering the surprise he has for her.

He takes out the small container with amber-colored hash balls in it.

He holds it up to the light. Shana looks at it impressed.

SHANA (CONT'D)
Is that it?

Shana takes it from him, opening the container for a closer inspection, smelling it.

OSCAR
Surprise.

Inside, small hash balls fill the container.

SHANA
Is it bubble hash?

Oscar shakes his head, "Nope."

OSCAR
We figured out how to make it do the ball thing.

Shana's eyes get big.

SHANA
So it's strong?

Oscar nods, "Yeah."

Shana looks at Oscar, smiling.

FLASHBACK TO.

INT. HOUSE/BEDROOM - NIGHT

Shana and Oscar sit at a trim table. Alone.

The trim table is on top of a tarp, catching the leaves. The bedroom is carpeted, light is scarce.

OSCAR
I think he's asleep.

SHANA
Keep a look out.

She packs a second zip lock bag full of pot. She wraps it up in a sweatshirt, putting it in her trim bag.

Shana looks at Oscar, "Done."

EXT. DRIVEWAY OF HOUSE - EARLY MORNING

Shana and Oscar exit a two-story house, walking through the landscaped yard.

They pause for a moment taking in the morning.

Sprinklers water the yard. They yawn, walking to the van.

The van pulls away, revealing a cookie cutter suburban neighborhood.

EXT. VAN - EARLY MORNING

The sun rises. Thin clouds fill the yellow and purple horizon.

Oscar drives down a country road toward the mountains. Shana sleeps in the passenger seat.

SHANA
(mumbling)
Wake me up when we get home.

Oscar yawns, focusing on the road.

EXT. OSCAR'S HOUSE, FRONT DOOR - EARLY MORNING

Shana stretches her arms to the sky.

SHANA
I'm not gonna' make it home. Can I crash on your couch?

Oscar nods, "Yeah," as the two stumble into the house.

INT. OSCAR'S BEDROOM - CONTINUOUS

Oscar points out the bed amidst the mess of his room.

> OSCAR
> You can have the bed. I'll take the couch.

Shana looks at him, "Seriously."

> SHANA
> (laying down)
> Just take the other side. I'll stab you if you try anything.

Shana drifts asleep as Oscar leaves the room.

INT. HALLWAY CLOSET - CONTINUOUS

Oscar opens the closet door, revealing a drying rack with multiple levels. All the levels are filled with weed.

He opens the zip lock bags, emptying the trimmed buds onto a rack.

He closes the door.

INT. BEDROOM - CONTINUOUS

Oscar lays on the other side of the bed, drifting to sleep.

Shana rolls over, putting her arm around Oscar. Tired.

Oscar opens his eyes, lying face to face with Shana.

She opens her eyes, staring into his eyes. Smiling.

They put their foreheads together, breathing the same air.

Shana slowly closes her eyes, falling asleep, snuggling into his chest. Home.

How to Kill a Bad Man

FLASHBACK END.

EXT. GROW SHACK WINDOW - DAY

Oscar and Shana put on rubber gloves.

They wipe down the tables, chairs, and every surface they touched with paper towels and alcohol.

INT. WAYNE'S BATHROOM - CONTINUOUS

Shana wipes down the toilet and sink.

INT. KITCHEN - CONTINUOUS

Oscar wipes down the counter tops, refrigerator, and sink.

INT. LIVING ROOM - CONTINUOUS

They wipe down table tops and all the door knobs.

INT. WAYNE'S HOUSE - CONTINUOUS

Shana and Oscar mop the floor. They're quiet.

>   OSCAR
> You know what I'm thinking?

>   SHANA
> How did this dumbass find this
> sweet house?

Oscar shakes his head, "No."

>   SHANA (CONT'D)
> How you don't ever want to be a
> grow ho?

Oscar smiles, "No."

>   OSCAR
> Where does Wayne hide his weed?

Shana scans the house, looking for hiding spots.

                    SHANA
          And cash.

Oscar looks at Shana, smiling.

INT. WAYNE'S BEDROOM - DAY

Oscar searches through drawers, flipping over clothes. Nothing.

He looks under the bed. Nothing

He scans the room, settling on the closet.

INT. WAYNE'S KITCHEN/LIVING ROOM - DAY

Shana opens and closes all the cabinets. Nothing.

She opens the last one, stopping.

                    SHANA
          Holy shi.....
               (eyeing the money)
          Oscar...Oscar...O.

Oscar appears, finding the money with his eyes. He's silenced by the stacks of cash.

                    OSCAR
          Holy shit.

INT. WAYNE'S BEDROOM - DAY

Shana and Oscar stare at something in the closet with their mouths gaping open.

Fifty bricks of weed, fifty pounds, is stacked in the closet.

Shana and Oscar look at each other. They get closer to the bricks of weed.

She smells it, smiling.

INT. KITCHEN/LIVING ROOM - DAY

Shana and Oscar put the money into a black trash bag.

The stacks are at least two inches thick, rubber banded together.

Shana picks up a stack, counting the bills.

> SHANA
> 1,000...2,000...4,000. This stack has 25 grand in it.

> OSCAR
> Is there enough for law school?

> SHANA
> How much is law school?

> OSCAR
> 100, maybe 300 grand.

Shana counts the stacks.

> SHANA
> 5..11...15...25...
> (grabbing extra stacks)
> There's 100...At least.

Shana tosses 5 stacks of cash at Oscar.

> SHANA (CONT'D)
> Enjoy law school.

Oscar laughs, packing up the cash.

EXT. WAYNE'S DRIVEWAY - AFTERNOON

They put the trash bag of money in the van.

EXT. SIDE OF WAYNE'S HOUSE - DAY

Shana and Oscar undress next to a faucet and garden hose.

They put their bloody clothes in a black trash bag.

Shana stands in her bra and panties as Oscar picks up the hose, handing it to Shana. He's in boxer briefs.

Shana looks at Oscar's body, smiling. Attracted.

>SHANA
>How come we didn't hook up that night?

Shana turns on the faucet as water comes out of the hose. She rinses her hands.

Oscar looks at Shana's tight body. Attracted.

>OSCAR
>I figured you were a "show kid," bent on drugs and goin' to music festivals...Just confused and running away.

>SHANA
>You thought I was a grow ho.

Oscar is quiet, guilty.

>OSCAR
>And then we started hanging out at lunch.

>SHANA
>And you thought I was a grow ho.

>OSCAR
>And then I met your dog and heard about your family.

>SHANA
>And then you realized...

>OSCAR
>I realized you're doing the best you can and you needed clarity. Not a guy.

Oscar looks at Shana.

>   OSCAR (CONT'D)
>   I wanted to be with you, but I
>   didn't want to fool you into
>   thinking you needed me.

Shana and Oscar pause, smiling at each other. Attracted.

>   OSCAR (CONT'D)
>   So, I told myself...Friends.

>   SHANA
>   And?

Shana finishes hosing herself off.

>   OSCAR
>   (smiling)
>   And you're not a grow ho.

Bloody water pours off Shana until it's clear.

>   SHANA
>   What if I don't go to California
>   this summer?

Oscar and Shana find each other's eyes.

>   OSCAR
>   If we get out of this, I'm
>   retiring. No more trimming.

She hands the hose to Oscar, thinking about it.

>   OSCAR (CONT'D)
>   Forever.

>   SHANA
>   (smiling at Oscar)
>   Forever.

Oscar puts the hose over his head, sending a shiver through his whole body as the blood washes off.

Shana and Oscar put on their extra clothes.

INT. WAYNE'S BEDROOM - DAY

Shana and Oscar pack the bricks of weed into various black trash bags.

Oscar pauses, holding a brick.

                    OSCAR
      So, you did want to hook up?

Shana stops, looking at him.

                    SHANA
    (smiling)
  I thought you were the type of guy
  who crushes on every girl he works
  with.

Oscar laughs to himself.

                  SHANA (CONT'D)
  But you never flirted with me...Or
  anything.

Oscar nods his head, agreeing.

                  SHANA (CONT'D)
  You didn't try to fool me by
  "worshipping the goddess."
    (pretending to be an
    enlightened hippie)
  All positive, love and light, peace
  be the journey shit.

Shana looks at Oscar, pausing.

                  SHANA (CONT'D)
  You were real. When you asked me
  to work homie's grows, you never
  took a cut. And you were a hard ass
  about the rate. It was cute.
    (pausing, thinking about the past)
  But you're right.
    (looking at Oscar)
  We're headed in different
  directions.

There's an awkward pause as they look at the bricks of weed, taking in the situation.

>   OSCAR
> Ever since we chopped up Wayne, our
> directions have started to...

Oscar holds up his hands, separately, slowly moving them together.

Shana slyly puts a brick in between his hands, stopping them from coming together. Oscar holds the brick, smiling at her.

Shana smiles back as they pack up bricks of weed.

EXT. REAR OF VAN - DAY

The rear van door is open.

They look at the van full of body parts, cash, and weed.

Oscar finds Shana's eyes, taking in the gravity of the situation.

He softly grabs her hand as their bodies get closer. Attracted. Finally. About to kiss.

A car APPROACHES in the drive way, interrupting the kiss. Hippie-jam band music POURS out.

Oscar and Shana hear the music, watching the car pull up. They look at each other, "We're fucked."

Oscar closes up the van, hiding the evidence.

CANDY, early 20's, parks the car, sticking her head out of the window.

>   CANDY
> (whiny, Southern accent)
> Is Wayne here?

>   SHANA
> He's not home.

CANDY
(getting out of the car)
Is the house open? I forgot my
charger last night.

Oscar looks at the front door. It's wide open.

OSCAR
Oh, yeah. Do you remember where it
is?

CANDY
I don't know. Maybe in the kitchen,
or maybe in the bedroom.

Candy walks into the house.

OSCAR
(following Candy)
We'll help you look for it.

SHANA
(following Candy and Oscar
into the house)
Let's look in the kitchen.

INT. KITCHEN - DAY

Candy and Shana search through the kitchen. Shana looks for a weapon.

Candy stops, thinking, scanning the kitchen.

CANDY
(whiny, Southern accent)
I can't believe it.

Shana finds a big knife and quickly hides it behind her back.

SHANA
Did you find it?

Candy is smelling the air.

How to Kill a Bad Man

>   CANDY
> No, but I think Wayne cleaned this
> place after I left.

Candy continues smelling the air, smiling to herself.

>   CANDY (CONT'D)
>   (looking at Shana)
> It smells clean. If a guy cleans up
> after you leave, he likes you.

Shana nods agreeing with Candy.

>   CANDY (CONT'D)
> Wayne and I met at a Red Rocks show
> on acid.

Candy turns to Shana.

>   CANDY (CONT'D)
>   (whispering)
> There are a lot of brokeasses out
> here and they'll try to trick you
> into "love, light, and..." whatever
> spiritual bull shit they use to
> control you.
>   (staring into Shana's
>   eyes, serious)
> That's why I stick with the older
> men. They know how to treat woman.

Candy holds up her right hand, rubbing her fingers together. The universal sign for, "Cash."

>   SHANA
> Totally.

>   CANDY
> You got to take care of you.

Shana holds the knife behind her back, nodding in agreement.

>   CANDY (CONT'D)
> Vaginas weren't born yesterday.

Candy stares down Shana, approaching like a hunter.

Candy gets closer...And closer...Invading Shana's space.

Shana is quiet, gripping the knife. Ready to kill this "grow ho."

Candy's nose is inches away from Shana's nose.

The knife slowly moves into stabbing position.

> CANDY (CONT'D)
> Did he try to fuck you?

The knife stops.

> CANDY (CONT'D)
> 'Cause that's mine.

Shana nods her head, "No."

> SHANA
> No, I just work for him.
> (whispering)
> Me and Tom are together.

Candy shifts her head, releasing the jealousy in her brow.

She notices the scrapes and bruises on Shana's face.

> CANDY
> None of my business, but you should find a man that cares.

Shana nods her head, "Yes."

> CANDY (CONT'D)
> (smiling)
> Don't waste your time.
> (scanning the room)
> I guess I got to buy another charger.
> (leaning in, whispering)
> I was hoping Wayne was here. Did he leave anything for me? Maybe some...

Candy makes the cash sign with her hand, again.

SHANA
(calling out)
Tom.

INT. WAYNE'S BEDROOM - CONTINUOUS

A phone charger appears, plugged into the wall.

Oscar grabs the charger, but stops before touching it.

SHANA (O.S.)
Tom. Did Wayne leave any money for Candy?

He looks for something to help pick up the charger without leaving fingerprints.

He finds a shirt on the ground, using it to grab the charger.

Oscar fumbles through his pockets, taking out the wad of cash.

OSCAR
(calling out)
Oh yeah, I forgot.

INT. KITCHEN - CONTINUOUS

Oscar enters the kitchen as Candy distances herself from him, "Asshole."

OSCAR
(holding up the charger)
Found it.

Candy looks at Oscar's hands as he gives her the charger.

She notices some redness, shooting him a dirty look.

OSCAR (CONT'D)
He left this for you.

Oscar hands her the wad of cash. Candy counts it out.

                             Josh Hyde

                    CANDY
            (smiling)
        I knew he liked me.

EXT. DRIVEWAY OF HOUSE - CONTINUOUS

Shana and Oscar watch Candy get into her car.

                    CANDY
            (hanging out the window)
        Tell Wayne to call me.

Candy rifles through her purse, finding a piece of blank paper.

She kisses it, leaving an outline of her lips on the paper.

She writes, "Candy - 618 521 1070."

She hands it to Shana.

                    CANDY (CONT'D)
        Just in case. Bye, y'all.
            (whispering into Shana's ear)
        You need to ditch him. You're too
        cute.

Candy looks at Shana, smiling, "Take care of yourself."

She makes eye contact with Oscar, shooting him a disgusted look, "Go fuck yourself prick."

The car pulls away, disappearing.

Shana relaxes, revealing the knife.

Oscar looks at the knife, finding Shana's eyes.

She hands him the knife, walking back into the house.

Oscar tosses the knife into the van.

INT. WAYNE'S BEDROOM - DAY

How to Kill a Bad Man

Shana and Oscar pick up the last two trash bags of weed.

EXT. DRIVEWAY OF HOUSE - DAY

Shana and Oscar carry the trash bags to the van.

They put them in, looking at each other, "We're almost done."

They get closer to each other. Attracted. About to kiss.

A phones BEEPS, announcing a text.

Oscar takes out Wayne's cell phone, flipping it open.

>   OSCAR
>   (reading the text message)
>   Driving down your road, now.

From a distance, a Dub Step beat APPROACHES as Oscar and Shana look around for the source.

Their eyes follow the BEAT to the driveway as an SUV approaches with shiny rims.

>   OSCAR (CONT'D)
>   We were so close.

Shana stares down the SUV.

The SUV pulls up, parking. The beat disappears as TWO SHOW KIDS, late 20's, white hippie gangsters, get out wearing sunglasses and flat-brimmed hats. They have full beards.

Oscar and Shana are calm. SHOW KID #1 and SHOW KID #2 walk up with swagger in their step.

>   SHOW KID #1
>   Yo, is Wayne here?

>   SHANA
>   Naw homie. He had an emergency and
>   wanted us to wait for you.

>   OSCAR
>   You're just picking up right?

Josh Hyde

Show Kid #1 looks at Show Kid #2. Suspicious.

              SHOW KID #2
       You know Wayne long?

Oscar smiles.

                 OSCAR
       Long enough.

              SHOW KID #1
       He likes to do things himself.

              SHOW KID #2
       Our boss likes to do things
       himself.

Show Kid #1 and Show Kid #2 look at each other, adjusting their shirts. Flashing gun handles.

Shana and Oscar look at the gun handles, silenced. A tense pause grows.

                 SHANA
         (smiling)
       You gonna' trade those for some
       weed?

Show Kid #1 and #2 are silent. Slowly, smiling at the joke.

              SHANA (CONT'D)
       I'll give you a pound for both of
       'em.

Show Kid #1 takes out his cell phone.

              SHOW KID #1
         (speaking into phone)
       Walkie Talkie app.

                 PHONE
         (coming out of the phone)
       Opening Walkie Talkie app.

Show Kid #1 and #2 wait for the app to open, posing with their arms crossed. Hard like 1990's gangster rappers.

Oscar and Shana look at each other, "Are these guys for real?"

The Show Kids stare down Shana and Oscar

>SHOW KID #1
>(talking into phone)
>T, he's not here.

>VOICE ON THE PHONE
>Who are they?

>SHOW KID #1
>Hold on...
>   (turning to Shana and Oscar)
>You guys got ID?

Shana and Oscar nod, "Yes."

Show Kid #1 and #2 put their hands on the guns.

>SHOW KID #1 (CONT'D)
>Slowly.

Shana and Oscar take out their badges. Slowly.

Show Kid #1 and Show Kid #2 see the badges, immediately at ease, taking their hands off the guns.

>SHOW KID #1 (CONT'D)
>You guys are badged?

Shana and Oscar nod, "Yes."

>SHOW KID #1 (CONT'D)
>Thank god. I hate all these cowboys.

>SHOW KID #2
>Sorry about the 90's gangers rap pose.
>   (re-enacting the pose)
>Can I borrow these?

Shana nods, "Go for it."

Show Kid #2 runs the badges to the SUV.

The back window rolls down as a hand takes the badges.

> TREE (O.C.)
> No fucking way.

A head pops out of the window. It's Tree, the tripping and rolling trimmer.

> TREE (CONT'D)
> Oscar...Shana.

Oscar and Shana look at Tree, getting out of the SUV. He has a gun holster, strapped across his chest.

Tree massively grins, waiving hello as he approaches. He hugs Shana and Oscar.

> TREE (CONT'D)
> I'm so happy it's you guys.

Tree looks around, making sure they're not being watched. He gives them the badges back.

> TREE (CONT'D)
> That Wayne guy is scary as fuck. He's a tweaker. How'd you guys meet?...Click and Clack.

> SHANA
> This is our first trim with homie.

> OSCAR
> He's dangerous and cray cray. He asked us to stay here, while he "went to run errands."

> SHANA
> He might be watching us from the woods just to see if he can trust us.

Shana leans into Tree as they all huddle.

> SHANA (CONT'D)
> (whispering)
> Cray cray.

> TREE
> (whispering)
> I only come up here 'cause it's cheap. I never get out of the car to make him think I'm important, but it's because I'm scared. These two guys are my younger brothers and that's my mom's car.

Tree smiles, pleased with himself.

> TREE (CONT'D)
> Nice cover right? You guys were scared like the hippie Bill Gates showed up.

> OSCAR
> Your brothers are scary.

> TREE
> Straight up ISIS on that ass. It's my Ganja-ihad.

Oscar and Shana laugh at Tree.

> TREE (CONT'D)
> Homie said he only had 5 pounds. Do y'all know if he has more?

Shana and Oscar nod, "He's got more."

> SHANA
> What do you need?

Tree thinks to himself, looking around, paranoid about Wayne watching.

> TREE
> (whispering)
> I got enough for like 15 or 25 bricks.

> OSCAR
> 22 for each.

Tree nods, "Yeah." Oscar smiles.

> OSCAR (CONT'D)
> I think he's got it.

Shana goes to the van, taking out three garbage bags of bricked weed.

She counts out the bricks, pulling out a couple extras.

Tree and Oscar watch her.

> TREE
> Thanks for the ride in the white buffalo. I'll never forget the colors man. It was like driving in a rainbow.

> OSCAR
> (smiling at Tree)
> The spirit world is a strange place.

Tree smiles back at Oscar as Shana drops 3 garbage bags in front of them.

Tree looks inside the garbage bags, counting out the bricks.

> TREE
> 5...12..20..25.

Tree looks at Shana and Oscar, grinning from cheek to cheek.

Tree SNAPS his fingers as Show Kid #1 and Show Kid #2 take stacks of cash out of their shorts.

They hand them to Tree.

Tree counts out $53,000. He hands it over to Shana and Oscar.

> TREE (CONT'D)
> Thanks guys.

Tree, Oscar, and Shana hug.

Tree SNAPS his fingers as his brothers load up the weed.

How to Kill a Bad Man

The SUV drives down the dirt driveway. Tree hangs out of the back window, waiving good-bye gun in hand.

                TREE (CONT'D)
Tatonka. Tatonka. Tatonka.

Tree FIRES a couple good-bye shots into the air.

Shana and Oscar watch the SUV disappear. Behind them, unnoticed, a UFO rises out of the trees, floating across the horizon, disappearing into the clouds.

                        FLASHBACK TO.

INT. FLOWERING ROOM IN A DISPENSARY WAREHOUSE - DAY

A large white room, 50 ft. by 50 ft., is filled with rows of cannabis ready to harvest.

Oscar and Shana are lost in the sea of green.

                SHANA (O.S.)
If you were a strain, which one would you be?

Big bug-eyed sunglasses protect their eyes from the high powered lights.

                OSCAR (O.S.)
Purple Thai because I'm sticky and if you get a piece of me, I'll blast you off to the moon...And I'm part Asian.

They both wear aprons as lanyards with Colorado Medical Marijuana Enforcement Division badges hang around their necks.

Oscar reaches into the sea of green, selecting the perfect bud to cut off.

The scissor tips cut the stem.

SHANA (O.S.)
I don't like this one, but I'm naturally this way. I'm euphoric, energizing, and narcotic.

Oscar tosses the bud in a full pan.

Shana smiles at Oscar.

SHANA (CONT'D)
I'm Chem Dawg.

Oscar smiles at her, picking up his pan.

OSCAR
I like the Dawg.

Shana picks up her pan. The two head toward the door.

OSCAR (CONT'D)
How many plants do you think we can do with one triminator?

SHANA
How many people do you think they're gonna' fire when we figure that out?

INT. TRIM ROOM - CONTINUOUS

There are a lot of NEW TRIMMERS around the table. GREG, late 60's, tall and on the edge of retirement, sits watching trimmers work. He doesn't trim. He supervises from the head of the table.

Shana and Oscar set the full pans on the table. Their sunglasses hang from their badges.

Click and Clack take some buds out of the fresh pans. They're wearing sunglasses, trimming extremely slowly.

CLICK
The machines make this so easy.

OSCAR
Is that why you're going so slow?

                    CLICK
        (whispering)
    Bro, I'm thinking about our jobs.
    Don't be the rabbit.

                    CLACK
    Be the turtle.

                    CLICK
    Slow and steady.

Click and Clack turn their heads in sync, looking at Oscar. Both of them nod at Greg.

                    CLACK
        (whispering)
    We're keeping an eye on him.

Greg eyes Oscar talking with Click and Clack.

Click and Clack notice Greg watching them. In sync, their hands reach for the pans of untrimmed buds, grabbing, and lifting them up above their heads.

                CLICK AND CLACK
        (British accents)
    Release the Kraken.

Click and Clack turn over the pans, dumping buds onto the table.

                    SHANA
        (looking at the table full
         of trimmers)
    Does any one want to harvest?

Click and Clack, quickly shake their heads, "No way."

                    CLICK
    I don't need to go to the beach
    today.

                    CLACK
    Definitely, no skin cancer for me
    today.

Josh Hyde

The table is quiet. Clack nods at the New Trimmers.

> CLICK
> (whispering)
> They're visitors. They'll get stuck in the net.

> GREG
> (Brooklyn accent)
> Hey, love birds. Keep harvesting for another hour and then I'll switch it up.

Shana and Oscar nod, "Thanks."

> GREG (CONT'D)
> Take these buckets to the machine.

Greg nods at two full 5 gallon buckets of untrimmed pot.

> OSCAR
> (British accent)
> To the triminator.

> GREG
> What'd we talk about?

Oscar and Shana shrug, "I don't know."

> GREG (CONT'D)
> It's not a terminator, it's not a "triminator." It's just a trim machine. It's like a big pair of scissors.
> (smiling)
> It has feelings, you know. It can hear you.

Oscar and Shana fake a smile, nodding their heads in agreement.

> SHANA
> Greg, you know machines don't have feelings? Right? Trimmers have feelings. We need to switch up the harvest team. The lights suck.

                    GREG
            (smiling)
        Okay, okay. I promise we'll switch
        it up soon.

Shana smiles, "Thanks."

                    GREG (CONT'D)
        Don't forget the buckets.

Shana and Oscar nod, "Yes," picking up two large 5 gallon buckets filled with buds.

Shana turns to Greg, leaning into his ear.

                    SHANA
            (whispering)
        These newbies have to learn the
        different stations and we have to
        rotate. Then you can fire whoever
        you want.
            (staring into his eyes)
        I'm not harvesting all day under
        the hot lights.
            (Brooklyn accent)
        Alright, love bird.

Greg's smile disappears as he nods, understanding.

Shana and Oscar exit, carrying the buckets.

INT. HALLWAY - CONTINUOUS

A shiny machine spins, making odd noises. Andrew looks at all the various parts, smiling. He's extremely high.

He notices Shana and Oscar approaching, carrying full buckets.

They set them down in front of the "triminator."

It looks like a large lawn mower with a large metal spinning tube.

Andrew pops into view.

                    ANDREW
            (Southern accent)
        What up ohmies? Ya'll wanna' see
        this thing triminate.

Shana and Oscar nod, "Sure."

                    ANDREW (CONT'D)
        Let's start this puppy up.

Andrew flicks a switch and a large canvas bag hooked up to a fan inflates like a punching bag.

                    ANDREW (CONT'D)
        The leaves are sucked up by the fan
        into the bag. Here's the cool
        part.

Andrew flips another switch on the "triminator," and the large metal tube begins to spin.

Andrew picks up a couple buds.

                    ANDREW (CONT'D)
        Shana, go to the other end and
        catch these.

Andrew drops a couple buds in the hole, leading to the spinning metal tube.

The buds spin through the tube, getting trimmed along the way.

Shana catches the trimmed buds, inspecting them. She smiles, impressed.

                    ANDREW (CONT'D)
        Not bad.

                    SHANA
        It's over.
            (looking at Andrew)
        Greg wants you to bring the empty
        buckets back to him.

Shana tosses the bud to Oscar.

Oscar tosses the bud in an empty 5 gallon bucket.

How to Kill a Bad Man

ANDREW
Is he our new boss?

Shana and Oscar nod, "Yeah."

ANDREW (CONT'D)
Why didn't any of us get the job?

OSCAR
They hired the old-new dude to
learn the system and fire us all.

SHANA
And they don't promote slaves.

ANDREW
Fucking Nazis.

Shana and Oscar nod, "Agreeing."

OSCAR
So…This thing gets covered in
scissor hash. Right?

Andrew grins, "Yes."

SHANA
(whispering)
Save it and we can make more hash.
(Brooklyn accent)
That Greg dude is clueless.

Andrew listens as his eyes get big, thinking about all the hash oil.

OSCAR
(Brooklyn accent)
Make sure you're the only one who
knows how to clean this thing.

Andrew smiles, nodding his head, "Yes sir."

SHANA
(Brooklyn accent)
Your new name is the Hash King.

                    OSCAR
              (Brooklyn accent)
          And you're from London.

Andrew smiles, stoned. Shana and Oscar walk down the hallway, stopping at the door to the grow room.

Shana and Oscar put their sunglasses on.

They open the door as an explosion of light pours out of the room, engulfing them.

                    SHANA
          I hate the beach.

                    OSCAR
              (Southern Accent)
          Fucking Nazis.

They disappear into the light.

INT. OFFICE - DAY

Click and Clack sit in a sparsely decorated office. There's a calendar, a set of metal shelves, some chairs, and a desk.

Greg sits at the desk.

                    GREG
              (Brooklyn accent)
          The machines are a lot faster than
          we thought. We won't need you two
          for the next harvest.

Click and Clack look at each other.

                    GREG (CONT'D)
          We'll give you a good reference and
          you have your badges.

Martin and Lucy sit across from Greg.

                    GREG (CONT'D)
          Since you're the oldest employees,
          we'll give you some extra money to
          help you transition.

Shana sits across the table from Greg listening.

> GREG (CONT'D)
> Thanks for the hard work.

> SHANA
> Are you gonna' keep any of us?

Greg is quiet, thinking of an answer. Oscar and Andrew sit across from Greg.

> GREG
> You're gonna' run the machines. And Oscar, I can give you a couple days a week.

Click and Clack look at Greg. Defeated.

Martin and Lucy sign non-disclosure agreements for Greg, exiting the office.

Andrew and Oscar sit across from Greg, absorbing the layoffs.

Shana looks at her badge and her scissors.

EXT. DISPENSARY, PARKING LOT - LATE AFTERNOON

Andrew carries a couple garbage bags out to a dumpster. He unlocks the dumpster, tossing the bags in.

He closes the dumpster, but doesn't lock the padlock. He disappears into the warehouse.

Shana and Oscar pull up in the white minivan. Shana jumps out, opening up the dumpster.

She grabs the two garbage bags, locks the dumpster, and jumps in the van.

EXT. BACK YARD - DAY

Martin, Click, and Clack dry out the hash on window screens.

They grind up dry hash into powder.

They load up a two-foot glass tube with hash powder.

A hand covers one end of the tube with coffee filters, rubber banding the filters around the tube.

Butane shoots through the glass tube, melting the hash powder into a liquid.

The liquid dissolves, leaving a hard amber sheet.

INT. KITCHEN - NIGHT

Martin, Andrew, Click, Clack, Oscar, and Shana break up and weigh the hash oil.

It's over a pound.

Shana smiles.

          SHANA
That's 10 grand.

INT. CAR - DAY

Oscar drives the van as Shana gives the pound of hash oil to a GRUNGY HIPPIE KID in the back seats.

The Grungy Hippie Kid hands her a stack of cash. Shana counts it.

          SHANA
It's 12. You're short.

The Grungy Hippie Kid hands her an extra stack of cash.

She counts it with speed and precision, smiling.

EXT. PARKING LOT - AFTERNOON

A white van sits parked overlooking mountains.

How to Kill a Bad Man

INT. VAN - CONTINUOUS

Martin, Click, Clack, Andrew, Oscar, and Shana smoke a joint in the van.

Shana hands out money to Martin, Click, and Clack.

                    SHANA
    It's about two grand a piece.

She counts out the rest of the money, giving it to Andrew and Oscar. She holds onto her money.

                    ANDREW
    I got more scissor hash.

Shana nods, "I can't."

                    SHANA
    I'm goin to Cali for the summer,
    but Oscar knows the guy now.

Oscar smiles at Andrew, "I'm in."

                    CLICK
    How's tomorrow?

Oscar, Martin, Andrew, Click and Clack smile at each other, "That works."

                                  FLASHBACK END.

EXT. MOUNTAIN TOPS - LATE AFTERNOON

Snow covered mountain peaks line the horizon.

A dirt road cuts through the tall peaks, partially hidden.

A van appears, leaving a trail of dust as the sun light calms the day.

EXT. VAN - CONTINUOUS

Oscar drives the van as Shana sits shotgun. Her face is scraped and bruised.

They are silent. Disheveled. Breathing slowly.

Exchanging glances, Oscar scans the horizon. Searching.

>   OSCAR
> I remember a pull off.

Shana's hands fidget. Nervous.

Oscar notices, softly grabbing her hands.

EXT. DIRT PULL OFF - CONTINUOUS

The van pulls off on a dirt road.

EXT. MOUNTAIN LOOK OUT WITH TREES - CONTINUOUS

A shovel hits the ground.

A pickaxe hits the ground.

Shana and Oscar dig a hole. It's the size of a human body.

The mountains surround them. Still.

EXT. VAN - CONTINUOUS

Multiple black trash bags are taken out of the back of the van.

EXT. MOUNTAIN LOOK OUT WITH TREES - CONTINUOUS

Shana and Oscar toss the trash bags into the hole.

They carry the last bag, struggling. It's the size of a human torso.

The hole is full.

Dirt is pushed into the hole, covering the bags.

Oscar looks at it. Not convinced.

Oscar walks around, searching for something. Shana watches him.

He picks up a rock, looks at it, "It's too small."

He tosses it aside, continuing to look.

He finds another rock, straining to pick it up. He smiles, walking toward Shana.

EXT. MOUNTAIN LOOK OUT WITH TREES - MOMENTS LATER

Stones cover the grave, concealing the fresh dirt.

Shana and Oscar sit on the pile of stones, staring at the horizon.

It's done.

The clouds reflect the sun as the sky unfolds.

                    OSCAR
No one is gonna' miss him.

Shana looks at Oscar, finding peace.

Oscar puts his arm around Shana, pulling her close.

Nestling into him, she feels safe.

EXT. VAN PARKED ON SIDE OF THE ROAD - CONTINUOUS

A police car is parked behind the van.

                POLICE OFFICER
I want to check the plates on a
White Toyota Minivan. License
Plate 751 YDA.

The POLICE OFFICER gets out of the car approaching the van.

Shana and Oscar walk on the trail, seeing the police car in the distance.

They get quiet, stopping.

Oscar and Shana look at each other, scared.

Shana puts the shovel and pickaxe behind a bush.

They approach the van, laughing, having fun as they see the Police Officer.

>POLICE OFFICER (CONT'D)
>Good afternoon. Are ya'll okay?

>OSCAR
>Yeah. We thought we saw a...
>(looking at Shana)
>A bear.

>SHANA
>And I wanted a photo of it. So we tried to find it.

>POLICE OFFICER
>Did you find it?

Oscar shakes his head, "No." He leans in, kissing the top of Shana's head.

>SHANA
>It was kind of scary. So we stopped looking...And we were...

Shana looks at Oscar.

>OSCAR
>And...We were making out.

The cop looks them up and down. They're a little dirty. Shana's face is scraped and bruised.

A BEEP announces a call on the radio. The cop pushes a button on his walkie-talkie.

>POLICE OFFICER
>What happened to your face?

Oscar and Shana look at each other, thinking of the words.

Shana smiles, laughing to herself.

      SHANA
  Tequila. I'm part Mexican.

The Police Officer LAUGHS with Shana.

     WALKIE TALKIE VOICE
  The plate is clear. Over.

      POLICE OFFICER
   (into walkie-talkie)
  Thank you. Over.
   (turning to Oscar and
   Shana)
  Well, ya'll be safe now.

The Police Officer smiles, walking back to his car.

     POLICE OFFICER (CONT'D)
   (opening his car door)
  Up the road about a mile, there is
  a great place you can...
   (smiling, thinking of the
   words)
  Watch bears from the car.

The Officer winks, smiling at the cute couple.

     POLICE OFFICER (CONT'D)
  Adios.

He gets in the car and drives away.

INT. VISTA OVERLOOKING MOUNTAIN ROAD - CONTINUOUS

The van is parked, surrounded by mountain peaks.

Shana, smiling, looks at the money. She counts the stacks of cash and looks at Oscar. The shovel and pickaxe are in the back seats.

                    SHANA
            I got something for you.

She takes out the piece of paper, handing it to him.

Oscar unfolds it, revealing Candy's lipstick kiss.

Oscar looks at Shana, smiling, getting closer to her lips.

The two kiss as it grows deeper, years in the making.

A phone VIBRATES, interrupting them.

They stop, finding each other's eyes.

Oscar checks his pockets, taking out the phone.

It's the text from Shana, "O, he's gettin' weird. Wait for me. PRACTICE IS OVER :-("

Oscar reads it to himself, looking at Shana, apologizing with his eyes.

                    OSCAR
            Sorry I was late.

Shana pulls Oscar into a kiss.

EXT. VISTA OVERLOOKING MOUNTAIN ROAD - CONTINUOUS

The mountain peaks watch over the parked van as Oscar and Shana continue making out.

Two bears can be seen on a distant mountain peak.

On the horizon a small UFO floats up, disappearing.

                                        FADE OUT.

Josh Hyde was born to a Filipino immigrant mother and American father. He graduated in film from Southern Illinois University in 2003. Hyde travelled to Peru to make a documentary on Peruvian shamanism, while interning at Kartemquin Films (*Hoop Dreams*, *Stevie*) and then entered the MFA program at Ohio University, working under Croatian director/producer, Rajko Grlic. He returned to Cuzco to shoot the short film, *Chicle*. (Berlinale, Tribeca, Hamptons), which was expanded into Hyde's first feature film, *Postales*. (Edinburgh, River Run, Shanghai, IFP)

Hyde helped shoot and edit the feature documentary, *Sweet Micky for President*, released by Showtime in 2016. (Slamdance, Hot Docs, EdgeFest, Los Angeles)

In 2017, Hyde wrote and directed his second narrative feature film, *My Friend's Rubber Ducky*. (RiverRun, Sun Valley, Midwest Independent)

Hyde enjoys hiking in mountains, a dry cappuccino, good street food, and chen style tai chi.

www.ingramcontent.com/pod-product-compliance
Lightning Source LLC
LaVergne TN
LVHW020935090426
835512LV00020B/3375